Amelia Earhart

A Photo-Illustrated Biography
by Marilyn Rosenthal and Daniel Freeman

Consultant:
Marilyn Copeland
Chairman of the
Amelia Earhart Birthplace Museum Board of Trustees
and former president of The Ninety-Nines, Inc.

Bridgestone Books
an imprint of Capstone Press
Mankato, Minnesota

Bridgestone Books are published by Capstone Press
151 Good Counsel Drive, P.O. Box 669, Mankato, Minnesota 56002
http://www.capstone-press.com

Library of Congress Cataloging-in-Publication Data
Rosenthal, Marilyn S., 1940–
    Amelia Earhart: a photo-illustrated biography/by Marilyn Rosenthal and Daniel Freeman.
    p. cm.—(Photo-illustrated biographies)
    Includes bibliographical references and index.
    Summary: A biography of the aviator and women's rights advocate who disappeared
while trying to fly around the world.
    ISBN 0-7368-0203-7
    1. Earhart, Amelia, 1897–1937—Juvenile literature. 2. Earhart, Amelia, 1897–1937—Pictorial
works—Juvenile literature. 3. Women air pilots—United States—Biography—Juvenile
literature. [1. Earhart, Amelia, 1897–1937. 2. Air pilots. 3. Women—Biography] I. Freeman,
Daniel B., 1920– II. Title. III. Series.
TL540 E3R67 1999
629.13'092—dc21
[B]   98-46103
                                              CIP
                                              AC

Editorial Credits
Chuck Miller, editor; Timothy Halldin, cover designer and illustrator; Kimberly Danger, photo
  researcher

Photo Credits
Archive Photos, 4
Corbis-Bettmann, 6, 8, 14, 16
The National Archives/Corbis, 10, 12, 18
New York Times Co./Archive Photos, cover

1 2 3 4 5 6 06 05 04 03 02 01

Table of Contents

"Because I wanted to."
–Amelia's answer to a reporter who asked why
she flew across the Atlantic Ocean alone, 1932

Famous Pilot

Amelia Earhart was the first woman to fly an airplane alone across the Atlantic Ocean. She also was the first person to fly alone across the Pacific Ocean.

Amelia used her fame as a pilot to help women. She founded a group for women pilots called The Ninety-Nines. Amelia was a career counselor for women at Indiana's Purdue University.

Most people remember Amelia for her last flight. She planned to fly around the world in 1937.

Amelia and her navigator, Fred Noonan, completed most of the trip. They were flying to Howland Island in the Pacific Ocean. Amelia made radio contact with the U.S. Navy. She told the navy that she and Fred were near the island. But they were almost out of gas. Then the navy lost radio contact.

The U.S. Navy sent airplanes and ships to search for Fred and Amelia. The navy never found them.

Amelia was the first woman to fly alone across the Atlantic Ocean. She was the first person to fly alone across the Pacific Ocean.

Childhood

Amelia was born July 24, 1897, in Atchison, Kansas. She had a younger sister named Muriel. Amelia's nickname for her sister was "Pidge."

Amelia's father, Edwin, was a lawyer for the railroads. Edwin traveled because of his job. Amelia's mother, Amy, traveled with him. Amelia and Pidge stayed with their grandparents in Atchison.

Amelia's grandmother wanted Amelia and Pidge to be ladylike. But Amelia and Pidge went fishing and played baseball. Most girls in the 1900s did not do these activities.

Amelia's parents and grandparents told her to stand up for her beliefs. Amelia and Pidge once freed the milkman's horse. They were upset because the milkman treated his horse poorly. Amelia and Pidge's grandmother did not punish the girls. Instead, she told the milkman to treat his horse better.

Amelia's grandmother cared for her during much of her childhood.

Education

Amelia's family moved often because of Edwin's job. The Earharts lived in Illinois, Iowa, Kansas, Minnesota, and Missouri during Amelia's childhood. Amelia attended many schools.

Amelia was a good student. Her favorite subjects in high school were chemistry and physics. She loved to read and write poems. Amelia graduated from Hyde Park High School in Chicago in 1915.

In 1915, most girls did not go to college. But one year later, Amelia went to the Ogontz School near Philadelphia, Pennsylvania. Amelia earned good grades at Ogontz. She was the vice president of her class. She also played field hockey.

But Amelia never graduated from Ogontz. Her plans changed when she visited Pidge in Canada in 1917.

Amelia became the first woman to fly across the Atlantic Ocean in 1928. She visited Hyde Park High School to talk about her flight.

9

New Interests

Amelia visited Pidge in Toronto, Canada, in 1917. Pidge was attending St. Margaret's College there. Amelia saw wounded soldiers returning from World War I (1914–1918). She wanted to help them.

Amelia took a job as a nurse's aide in a military hospital in Toronto. Many of the patients were pilots. Amelia was interested in their stories about flying.

In 1919, Amelia returned to the United States. She studied to be a doctor at Columbia University in New York. But she never forgot about flying.

In 1920, Amelia moved to Los Angeles to live with her parents. She planned to continue medical school there. Amelia went to an air show shortly after she arrived. Edwin paid for Amelia to take a ride in an airplane. Amelia's interest in flying became stronger. Amelia quit medical school. She decided to become a pilot.

Amelia's visit with Pidge (pictured at left with their mother) in Toronto helped her decide to become a nurse's aide.

Becoming a Pilot

Amelia took her first flying lessons from Neta Snook. Neta was one of the few licensed women pilots in the world. In 1922, Amelia received her pilot's license.

Amelia's mother and sister helped Amelia buy her first airplane. It was a yellow biplane. A biplane is an airplane with two sets of wings. Amelia began performing in air shows with her biplane.

Amelia set a new women's altitude record at an air show in 1922. Amelia's airplane climbed 14,000 feet (4,267 meters) into the air before its engine stopped. Amelia landed her airplane safely.

In 1924, Amelia's parents divorced. Amelia sold her airplane so she could buy a car. Amelia drove her mother to Boston where Pidge now lived.

Amelia found a job as a social worker in Boston. She counseled young children. But Amelia did not stop flying. She went flying in her free time.

Amelia learned to fly in California and kept flying after she moved to Boston.

Friendly Flight

In 1928, Amelia met with book publisher George Palmer Putnam. He was arranging an airplane flight across the Atlantic Ocean. The airplane *Friendship* belonged to Amy Guest. She wanted to show that women could fly in airplanes like men could.

George wanted Amelia to be a passenger on the flight. She would be the first woman to travel across the Atlantic Ocean in an airplane. On June 17, 1928, Amelia, pilot Wilmer Stultz, and a mechanic took off from Newfoundland, Canada. They landed safely near England 20 hours and 40 minutes later. Amelia instantly became famous. But she did not feel she had earned the fame. She had not been the pilot.

George became Amelia's manager after the flight. He arranged for her to write books and give talks about flying. Amelia and George became friends. They married in 1931.

George and Amelia were partners in business and in life. George asked Amelia to marry him several times before she said yes.

New Records

Amelia was famous because of the *Friendship's* flight across the Atlantic Ocean. But she wanted to set a record by herself. She wanted to fly across the Atlantic Ocean alone. No woman had done this.

By 1932, she was ready to make the flight. Amelia would fly a Lockheed Vega. The airplane could carry enough fuel to fly 3,200 miles (5,150 kilometers) without stopping.

On May 20, 1932, Amelia took off from Newfoundland, Canada. Her airplane's altimeter quit. Amelia could not tell how high she was flying. She also had to fly through heavy rain and strong winds. But she landed safely in Ireland 13 hours later.

Amelia wanted to become the first person to fly nonstop across the Pacific Ocean. Ten pilots had died attempting this flight. In 1935, Amelia took off from Hawaii and landed safely in Oakland, California.

Amelia broke many women's flight records in her Lockheed Vega.

"There's just about one more good flight left in my
system, and I hope this trip around the world is it."
–Amelia to a reporter before her flight around the world, 1937

Women's Rights

Amelia used her fame to help women. She started The Ninety-Nines in 1929. This group of women pilots originally had 99 members. Today, The Ninety-Nines continues to encourage women to become pilots.

Amelia knew U.S. President Franklin Delano Roosevelt and his wife, Eleanor. Amelia and Eleanor gave speeches in favor of women's rights.

The president of Purdue University, Edwin C. Elliot, was impressed with Amelia's efforts. Edwin asked Amelia to become a career counselor at Purdue. Amelia advised almost 1,000 women students.

At Purdue, Amelia began planning a flight around the world. She wanted to be the first person to fly around the earth near the equator. Purdue helped pay for an airplane that could fly 4,500 miles (7,242 kilometers) without refueling.

Amelia helped build the Lockheed Electra she used in her attempt to fly around the world.

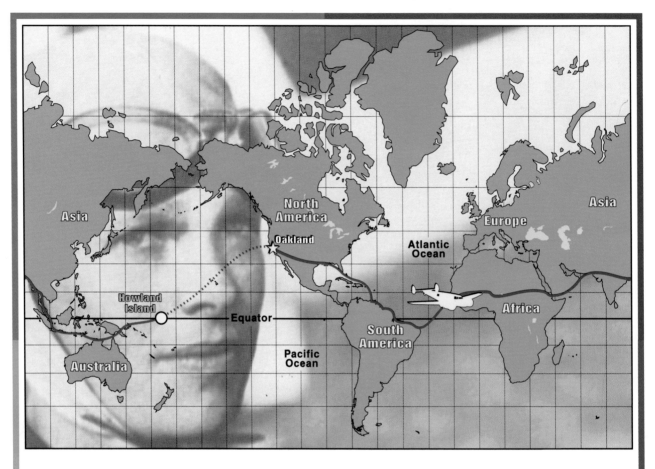

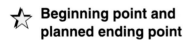
Amelia Earhart's Last Flight

On May 21, 1937, Amelia and navigator Fred Noonan left Oakland, California. They flew to Miami, Florida, making several stops along the way. Amelia wanted to make sure the airplane was working properly before leaving the United States. Amelia and Fred flew more than 22,000 miles (35,405 kilometers) in the next six weeks. But on July 2, Amelia and Fred disappeared near Howland Island in the Pacific Ocean.

Final Flight

On June 1, 1937, Amelia and her navigator, Fred Noonan, took off from Miami, Florida. They made stops in South America, Africa, Asia, and Australia.

On July 1, Amelia and Fred took off from Lae, New Guinea. Their last stop before arriving back in the United States was Howland Island. This tiny island in the Pacific Ocean was 2,500 miles (4,023 kilometers) northeast of Lae.

But Amelia and Fred never made it to Howland Island. Amelia lost radio contact with the U.S. Navy at around 8:45 A.M. on July 2. She had told the navy they were near the island. She said the airplane was almost out of gas. Amelia and Fred had disappeared.

Ships and airplanes searched 250,000 square miles (647,500 square kilometers) of ocean for 15 days. Amelia and Fred were never found. No one knows why Amelia's airplane disappeared.

No one has been able to solve the mystery of Amelia and Fred's disappearance. Their airplane was never found.

Fast Facts about Amelia Earhart

 One of Amelia's nicknames was Lady Lindy. Amelia looked much like famous pilot Charles Lindbergh.

 Amelia was awarded the National Geographic Society's Gold Medal for her transatlantic flight.

 The route Amelia planned to take around the world covered more than 27,000 miles (43,451 kilometers).

Important Dates in Amelia Earhart's Life

1897—Born July 24 in Atchison, Kansas
1917—Becomes a nurse's aide at a hospital in Toronto, Canada
1919—Moves to New York; begins medical school
1920—Moves to Los Angeles; begins flying lessons
1922—Gets her pilot's license; buys her first airplane
1928—Flies across the Atlantic Ocean as a passenger on the *Friendship*
1929—Helps start The Ninety-Nines, a group of women pilots
1931—Marries George Palmer Putnam
1932—Becomes the first woman to fly alone across the Atlantic Ocean
1935—Becomes the first person to fly alone across the Pacific Ocean
1937—Disappears near Howland Island in the Pacific Ocean

Words to Know

altimeter (al-TIM-uh-tuhr)—a gauge that tells a pilot how high off the ground an airplane is flying

biplane (BYE-plane)—an airplane with two sets of wings; one set of wings is above the other set of wings on a biplane.

career counselor (kuh-RIHR KOWN-suh-lur)—someone who helps another person choose a job or career

equator (e-KWAY-tuhr)—an imaginary line that runs around the center of Earth

navigator (NAV-uh-gay-tuhr)—someone who plans an airplane's flight path; navigators read maps for pilots.

social worker (SOH-shuhl WUR-kur)—someone who provides financial or educational support to those who need it

Read More

Davies, Kath. *Amelia Earhart Flies around the World.* Great 20th Century Expeditions. New York: Dillon Press, 1994.

Kerby, Mona. *Amelia Earhart: Courage in the Sky.* Women of Our Time. New York: Puffin Books, 1992.

Szabo, Corinne. *Sky Pioneer: A Photobiography of Amelia Earhart.* Washington: National Geographic Society, 1997.

Useful Addresses

Amelia Earhart
   Birthplace Museum
223 North Terrace Street
Atchison, KS 66002

The Ninety-Nines, Inc.
   International Headquarters
Box 965
7100 Terminal Drive
Oklahoma City, OK 73159

Internet Sites

Amelia Earhart
http://www.ellensplace.net/eae_intr.html
The Ninety-Nines—International Organization of Women Pilots
http://www.ninety-nines.org
The Official Site of Amelia Earhart
http://www.ameliaearhart.com

Index